<u>Scream</u>

Tear your flesh,

Cry your tears,

Scream, it's all in vain.

Realize despite

your twisted hopes,

This is no longer

Your domain.

The lights went out,

The town went dark,

Empty now the streets

Hideous day,

No one to see,

Except THE ONES YOU MEET.

Discarded, destroyed,

And yet

I smile,

Sorrowful,

this joy,

It bleeds me dry

I've succumbed again,

Suffering; it's yours

Enjoy.

<u>*Dessert*</u>

Have your slice of humble pie,

Feed your wicked face.

Perchance you've been here before?

Have you visited this place?

This place inside my tortured mind

So many twists and turns.

An endless pleasure in and of itself,

But entry must be earned.

I'll take your love,

Set it aside,

Break your fucking heart.

Then circle back,

It's another day

Where, love, would you like to start?

Conflicting lies

Breath on my thighs

I've got this under control,

When you were here

Forgot my fear,

And my life as a whole.

I take you in,

Repeat my sin

Over and over,

Repeat,

This lie of a life,

This goddamned strife

The end and my self meet.

<u>*Count the ways*</u>

How many ways

Can you find

To break my broken spirit?

How many times

Have I told myself,

Do you think I need to hear it??

Insults flung in

Fits of rage,

Always at my expense.

Your love of me, a mockery,

Does that make any sense?

Such anger, such disdain,

While I sit encased in fear

As you break me and all for which I care

All the things I hold dear.

My sanity is broken,

My self respect is gone,

You've taken the things I worked for

And any chance of things I want.

Someone tell her

Someone *get her up,*

You are on the white side, I am on the black side,

Now would be a good time…..

<u>Accusing</u>

Accusations

That take my breath,

Unfeeling nature,

I long for death.

This knife is yours,

Please take it back,

Leave me alone,

I know the things I lack.

Your hate filled eyes,

And all these lies,

Tomorrow

Begins

Now.

<u>*Nothing*</u>

Antagonistic views sent forth

My values, what I'm worth.

Piss on me, make a mockery,

Of anything I will ever be.

Answer to the voice of one,

Who condescends yet IS NO ONE.

You think you're more, I'll tell you now,

With this admit, with this avow

I will rise above,

Forget your "name,"

Your view of me, your obvious disdain,

I've got your pain, I've felt much more,

And this is all you must endure?

It must be nice, that's all you feel?

When I question each day my sense of real?

If you want some pain

I'll provide you with,

More pain than you could vanquish.

At this point I LONG TO DIE

I'm nothing in your condescending eyes.

<u>Retribution</u>

I hope one day pain eats into your soul

I hope you wake in pieces, Not even almost whole.

I hope one day the life you live crumbles,

Though you try to stay straight,

You fall, you stumble.

I hope your face is rubbed in all of YOUR mistakes,

I hope your life by your own hand you wish to take.

I hope your pain takes over

Claims your sanity,

I want you to imagine

That for one day

YOU'RE ME.

<u>*Colorful*</u>

What do you want with me?

Another end, can you not see?

Will I ever truly, madly, deeply be?

Will I continue to be insane?

And what defines "insanity"

Whatever color do YOU decree???

<u>*Moment to Moment*</u>

Insatiable dominance

Unaltered dreams

What a disgrace I have become

This life isn't what it seems

One moment you feel lonely

Next moment, loved so true,

One second colors shine so bright

Next moment

A shade of blue.

<u>*Let it Be*</u>

Let this be a nightmare from which one day I'll wake,

Let the lies disappear, please this sadness take.

Let the light come shining through, let the clouds be gone,

Let this be a lesson to me, let the truth be known.

Let my smile return to me, the one you used to love,

Let my bitterness just float away, far, far up above.

Let my heart be pure, my God, let my self be true,

Let me stray from this evil life, let me good things do.

Let my paranoia prove to be in my mind,

Let me see the good in me,

Let there be some left to find.

Paid In Full

I pay your will with an act of grace,

To see the light shine on your face,

While my lives seem numbered, in sorrow laced,

Inundation of burning tears.

I beg of you, please hold me now,

You hurt me, yes, but anyhow,

I won't move on, I won't allow

Tomorrow to foreshadow fears.

Because to move on brings opposition of bliss,

My solace is your tainted kiss,

I know nothing, but I do know this,

There is no escaping here.

Promises, Promises

A promise made, a fucking lie,

Into this, fade, do you deny?

Your accusations prove untrue,

Your grace denied, my soul left blue.

My ignorance, tried and true,

My intent I give it back to you.

Your love on a timer that's run out,

My mind is faded, filled with doubt,

I want to know, how can you now,

Disregard all of yesterday's vows?

Who the fuck do you think you are?

I wished and wished,

God damn that star.

It's a game, a joke, a mockery of me,

And you will JUST REFUSE TO SEE?

We'll see tomorrow what lives on,

We'll see who sings the happy songs.

And until then your soul should bleed,

Until then you'll know true greed,

Until then on your addiction feed,

I know this,

I'm MORE THAN YOU.

<u>*It's OVER now*</u>

Punished for lack of conformity,

Subservience you seek?

Lost my self when I found you,

You broke me, made me weak.

The days are gone of taking,

I can only take so much.

Control is lost,

Trust shattered,

Ruined by your jaded touch.

Take this pain and feel it,

I hope it breaks you, too.

Take this anger and deal with it,

For me, it's nothing new.

So lost so long so confused-

Happy?

What does that mean?

You've redefined my every fear,

Broken all my dreams.

I know now what's been missing here.

<u>*Reminisce*</u>

Every word a reminder,

Of stupid mistakes of past,

Each sickening moment

Of each fucking day

An eternity does last

My ignorant smile amuses you?

You think it's funny to have faith?

I'll take your smile,

I'll show you pain,

Your innocence I'll rape.

You said you'd be there

And you were not,

My doubts intensify,

I hate me now,

I hate my face,

Hate these stupid, weakened cries.

I've searched my self, I came up short,

Who took advantage? Who???

I'm without a soul, apparently

And I'm clueless...

What to do???

<u>Live It Up</u>

Smoke your dope

Drink your beer,

Whatever makes it fade

I'd love to hear your cold advice

When it a difference made.

I'll take my pride, what's left of it

And hand it over to you,

I'll disregard your opinion

About everything I do.

You said that you would love me

You said you'd be there when,

I had no one, yet here we go

Your solution? Condescend.

I know that I've made my mistakes

Shall we reflect on yours?

No I don't wish to cause you pain

Don't wish to portray disdain,

That's certainly not the cure.

A hug was missed, an "It'll be okay"

A heart breaks even now,

And again you repeat the same mistakes

Yet I have made myself a vow.

I shall move on from here,

I shall digress no longer,

My broken heart will be my strength,

What doesn't kill us makes us stronger.

<u>*Lucky*</u>

Some of you are getting lucky

Others cling to misery

-It's safe here

They know my name-

Shadowed figures you can't see.

Don't worry I've got you

Don't worry, I've got you

Don't worry, I've got you

<u>*DON'T WORRY, *</u>

<u>*I'VE GOT YOU*</u>

<u>*Better*</u>

You said you'd make it better,

You said you'd love me despite,

My flaws and my insanity,

And the fact that I'm not quite,

Your average normal everyday

Girl, I'm complicated,

You should have taken the time to see,

If only you'd have waited.

You would have seen what I am going to be,

I'll show you who I am

I'm make sure, consequently

That my life is worth a damn.

Feel the overwhelming pain?

Feel the tugging of your heart?

Do you feel it breaking in half?

Did you notice

How it almost kills?

Can you imagine,

Now,

Why I act the way I do,

Unable to deal?

I beg for you to go,

You refuse.

In this house of ill repute

My anger begins to grow

Such violent thoughts

You decline?

Respond with bitter screams?

I have asked before

And now I beg,

Don't let me be the way I seem.

I feel all alone

Even when you're here,

I need someone to HELP

Can't you just fix it for me?

<u>*A Name*</u>

And you think you can just come back in,

I should disregard all your sins?

You think you're cool, this will not do,

Fuck your lies your intent untrue.

Your conformity,

Your lack of trust,

Your demise I crave,

Mandatory, a must.

You are nothing now, a joke to me,

I'm a bitch?

Just wait and see.

Your childish game

Will get you still,

Against your NAME

Against your will.

You'll learn the true meaning of PAIN

Perhaps you too will go insane.

<u>***Whatever It takes***</u>

Convince yourself it isn't you

It's everyone else in the world,

Convince yourself you're better,

Not this stupid, bitter girl.

Convince yourself that IT'S OKAY,

The bad will disappear,

Convince yourself you're strong enough,

To face this toxic fear.

Convince the world that you're the same,

The one they knew before,

You're good enough, you'll make it work,

You can and will endure.

Convince yourself you deserve the best,

It will come for you in time,

Convince yourself your sanity

Is still present in your mind.

Convince yourself you can play their games,

Convince yourself you'll win,

Convince yourself you've done no wrong,

This too shall pass, my friend.

Beautiful Dreamer

Your words are rose petals,

They slide right off your tongue,

Lust I do,

For the past, for you,

For days when I was young.

Too bad of late I'm older,

Your words are so much colder,

And when I had the chance should I

Have forgiven you, let sleeping dogs lie?

Let you break me down,

Spit in my face?

Remind me of my horrid disgrace?

I hope you bleed, feel it deep inside,

Beauty polluted with all your stupid lies.

<u>Yesterday</u>

And you condescend, you do my friend,

Might I show you now to your dark end?

Might I interest you in what has, what's been?

Might I murder your self control?

And my wounds don't bleed so much, no doubt,

How did I really go without?

Your wicked deception, my subliminal clout?

Will I ever be a person? Whole?

Where went the promises of yesterday?

Where went the sun, why skies, so gray?

Deviation divine, my doubt, I strayed,

Whatever once was mind, you stole.

And here you come again, those words,

So bittersweet, maddeningly absurd,

It all turned bad, your love curdled,

Not to hate, that would be my goal.

<u>A Joke</u>

Across the waves of yesteryear,

Everything darkens,

The end is near,

Your lack of love, it fuels my fear,

Contradiction left you hope.

A love divine, a foreign dope,

You make me real, my thoughts provoked.

Once our love was new

Now it's faded away, distance, it grew.

How sad.

<u>*Morning Glory*</u>

I get up in the morning,

I cannot explain why,

These thoughts that echo in my head,

Make me long to die.

I cling to past decisions,

Stupid, foolish girl,

I want to kill the crowds of you

And everyone else in the world.

<u>*dumb*</u>

Clouded visions lie

Within my cluttered mind,

Reason lost,

No explaining why.

Solution? I cannot find.

Ask again I'll say the same,

Can't deny the truth,

Reach into the past

To hold onto

Some semblance of my youth

Insanity, it's in my veins,

Lies inside my head,

Longing for….

I can't recall,

Would I be better dead?

There is no why

There is no how

There is no moving on

When you wake up

And reach for me,

I will be gone.

<u>*Insomniac*</u>

Insomniac,

Restless mind,

What secrets do I hope to find?

When dark turns light,

Then Back again

See my flaws, I cannot pretend,

To be someone

Other than me,

Though easier

My life would be.

Tainted versions of myself

Lead to spite

And thirst for death.

<u>*Imagine*</u>

Imagine this

A soul divine,

Kisses so sweet

They blow your mind

Entity created

Just for me,

Alone again,

I wake I see.

Where were you then?

Where are you now?

You broke my heart,

I do avow.

Despite this,

Please give me again,

Blessed wretched

Beautiful sin

Shake me to the very core

Give me some more.

Supply the very air I crave

So cowardly

Yet you call me brave?

I Step into your cluttered mind

Where shadows fear to tread,

Sick versions of my self come forth

I wake the sleeping dead

Raindrops clinging to my face,

Soaked now to the core,

You scream, I cry, the lightning strikes

I beg you now for more.

You speak in verse I comprehend

Your touch brings clarity,

Divides the pain and speaks the truth

A gift from you to me.

Tell me now of sunlit dreams

And discoveries of now,

Forgive the past,

Forget the pain,

This be our solemn vow.

<u>Where?</u>

Deception, where lies now your self?

Solitude is bliss,

Blinded by my tainted ways

Enemy's grave kiss.

The sun, it hides it's bitter face

Refuses to be seen,

Obsession with my agony,

Beauty so obscene,.

Travelling this endless road,

Nowhere left to go

My clarity lost, can't be replaced,

The end is all I know.

Misfortune, bleak and cold and lost,

Forgive me for my sins,

Blood turns cold,

Fade to black

And then we start again.

<u>*In Your Mind*</u>

Test my faith

Make me bleed,

Innocence torn to shreds,

Moonlit cries of yesteryear,

Cannot escape my head.

Psychotic screams

Echo within

The confines of my soul,

Lost years, lost life

Let me breathe

Give to me control.

Of life, of love, of here, of now,

Of everything I lost,

Forgive me,

Smile now, beautiful

The overwhelming cost.

Repeat the past,

Forget your name

I drown inside these tears,

I lost, again, my time is up

Though dismissed I linger here.

Disillusioned

Bleeding remorse

Eats into

The sanity of now,

Dark visions emerge

From a tainted mind,

Questioning just how,

This life became

A maze of sorts

To which there is no end,

Forget my pride

Fade to black,

Don't love just condescend.

Faith is gone,

Tomorrow a day

That's promised but to few,

Won't wake to see,

Won't deal with this,

I need now something new.

Greed

Greedy disposition,

The soul that keeps you here,

Waiting to no avail

Where have you been, my dear?

It's been a while, I've been afraid,

Assuming you've moved on?

Whatever was left of your memory

Now, forever gone.

Forget your lies, forget your love;

You'll get what you deserve.

Place my heart in danger,

Trample on my nerves.

Blindside my heart, you are to blame,

You refuse closure

I've had my share

Know how this ends

This is far from over.

No one here gets out alive

<u>*Shaken*</u>

Seeing red, it eats me alive

Cannot stop this shaking

A joke of me, that's what you've made,

I'm sick and tired fo taking

All these games,

So fun for you

So hurtful though to me,

I've had too much

Can't take much more

When will this end, I see?

One more time,

One more call,

I've been pushed too far already,

Can't control my rage,

Cannot keep it straight,

Cannot keep it steady.

<u>*Sunset*</u>

The sun sets on another day

Chalk up, now, your loss,

Despite the entity of hate

Despite what this life costs.

I'll know your name

When the time doth come,

I'll see your torrid fear.

Know me now, long for then,

Hold me, please, my dear.

<u>*Questioning*</u>

Where were you when things fell apart?

Who was I supposed to love?

Where were you when I longed for death?

Just somewhere up above?

I hope to you that you'll prove true,

I hope you'll make some sense,

I hope you'll bring clarity my way

And from those lies, repent.

I want to believe in something,

I want to believe in you,

And yet I keep on failing

At everything I do.

I've heard if I believe in this

Everything will turn out fine,

I hear that if I sense your voice

Forgiveness will be mine.

It's impossible, I hate myself,

For all the doubt inside

Why can't the truth just come forth?

Must it always hide?

Clarity, where is it? Where?

Where is this alleged light?

Perchance the beauty of your name

Will eliminate this fight?

WHERE ARE YOU??

<u>Who's sorry?</u>

Sit in judgment, no true remorse,

My heart will heal,

Life takes it's course.

Ripped away, mistakes brought back

Excluded from them,

Pride under attack.

What have I left,

Please HELP ME OUT

I want those things

I'm left without.

How do you live

With the self you chose

So full of denial

Yet everyone knows.

The reality of you,

It's in your eyes,

Deny your life,

Unconvincing your lies.

Perverse, this sin,

You've held within

You cry aloud,

Alone in a crowd,

Where faces blur,

Cannot concur,

The how the why,

Is it wrong to try?

To smile to laugh

Follow their path,

To incomparable bliss,

A demonic kiss.

Melancholy Smile

Now, as in the past

These days won't last

Disasters unfold

Things left untold,

All things aside,

To run, to hide,

You must stay here,

To quench my fear,

Sadness steals my smile,

Make this life worthwhile.

If you've imagined it can't get much worse

Or thought this ache the last,

Prepare yourself for thrice as bad,

Than anything that's passed.

If you thought yourself untouchable,

Thought yourself too good,

Perhaps you should redefine your hell,

Everybody should.

You haven't even begun this tour,

You have so much left to learn,

Your "friends" were all imagined

Their trust you never earned.

Know that all the things you loved

Can be snatched from your pitiful hand,

Know that you are nothing,

No one will meet your sick demands.

Know that change will do no good,

Yesterday will always be,

So try as you might you won't escape

You're you, inevitably.

<u>*Mother*</u>

Shallow breathing, I've lost my light,

I can barely hear my heart,

I hold you close, yet far away,

I scream as you depart.

I thought this sacred thing was mine,

I thought to me you could cling,

I prayed that despite the hard truths of life,

I'd to you, safety bring.

I thought I prayed I realized

Who I was despite it all,

I overcame, I fell again

I heard you when you called.

I made you real, I molded you,

Provided you with love and care,

I felt your weakness, kissed your fears,

Made life easier to bear.

When did I become a threat to you,

When did they decide

To rip us apart, to break my heart,

To stomp on what was left of my pride?

I'll be the one you knew before,

I'll come back, I'll make you see,

That for eternity, despite mistakes of old,

A mother to you I will be. *(I'm sorry...)*

Weak

The doubt is evident in your eyes,

The truth is in your voice,

You consider me incompetent,

Did I ever have a choice?

Left wondering which path to take,

Too many times been wrong,

Perhaps with reassurance,

you'd have proven much more strong.

I told the truth despite the cost,

Begged on hands and knees,

You lost your life, your everything,

The moment you could not seize.

Naked, shivering, void of truth,

Dementia overcame,

Needed too much, realized too late

Had no one left to blame.

You took your fate in your own hands,

Too proud to admit mistakes.

Took and took until you became void,

Now there's nothing left to take

<u>*More*</u>

I wish that you could know me now

I wish the stars would fall,

I wish that fate had smiled on you,

I truly gave you my all.

I wish that you could climb into

This mind and just know me,

I wish that you could hold me now,

I wish that you could see.

I need you, I'm broken inside,

One day they'll see my worth

I know a million apologies

Won't fix what you deserved.

I want to hold you in my arms,

I want you, please, back here,

Why can't I just take it back?

Why couldn't it have been more clear?

I'm sorry for your weakness

You needed more than I,

Every time I think of you, Inside I slowly die.

Forgive me, Father, for I have sinned,

I pray you ache no more,

You just couldn't bring yourself to love,

Life was too much to endure.

<u>*Cannot*</u>

I could not delve into your head,

I could not read your mind,

I could not make your decisions,

I could not for you peace find.

I had my babies, myself,

Now I'm weaker than before.

I have no one on whom to lean,

It's so much to endure,

Can you help, can you guide me?

This is all I ask.

Just watch us here

From way up there,

Can you complete this task?

Please

<u>*Step In*</u>

In steps the mind that outward knew,

The things of old, what else to do?

Where went the days of yesteryear,

Nothing to know, nothing to fear.

Forget the pain, forget the loss,

They've never been worth the peace they cost.

My sanity, my youth, my love

My ability to rise above.

Forget me now, I'm nothing then,

Repeated mistakes, retribution for sin.

<u>Disaster</u>

In a massive display

Such disarray,

Chaos from order

Always on the border

Of neurotic dissension

Did I fail to mention?

Life turns the bend,

Once again god sends,

Misery my way

Can't go, must stay.

Sanctioned remorse

Life takes it course,

And we're again at the start

With so broken a heart.

Again.

<u>*Back Then*</u>

Elaborate deception

The life you used to live,

Fragments, bitter pieces,

Are all you had to give.

This goes on and on,

And now you're gone.

Things appear so grave,

Yet I have to be brave.

Fed up with the lies,

My soul doth cry,

My jaded doubt,

Incomplete without,

Should have cleaned the slate

Now it's too late.

Cling always to this concept,

The mind tends to forget

The weak find reason to lose the fight

It's much easier to quit.

<u>Simple</u>

Unforgivable intentions,

Deceiving reality,

Forced to kneel at their command,

Forced by the blind to see.

Follow the path of righteousness,

In their shadows find your name,

Our entity cursed, your pride raped,

Individuality equals shame

Hide your face in the bitter night,

Refuse to know the day,

Colors never cling to you,

Life so dark and gray.

Sorrowful happiness,

Solitude you seek,

Words stick painfully in my throat,

Is it safe, yet, to speak?

Who knows what secrets would unfold,

If honesty set in,

Who knows what revelations of past

Would come erupting from within?

It's best to hold your tongue now,

It's easier, you know

To keep it all locked inside,

Simply allow the pain to grow.

Don't allow the world to know your fear,

You're not allowed to cry,

You'll be punished for intervention,

Just give up asking why.

<u>*Reassurance*</u>

Store up the pain of yesteryear,

Throw away the key,

No complications, no questions left,

About this entity.

Deny your passions,

Deny your love,

Complications are not the norm,

Shamed for being different,

From the moment you were born.

Take the road less traveled

And surely you will fail,

Take the truth to heart at last,

Things won't turn out well.

Resentment breeds chaotic bliss,

Anger through the years,

A hatred not quite human,

Though morbid, it stays here.

Never confident, never reassured,

The one you needed failed,

Take the blame within yourself,

Another sad and twisted tale.

Change

I'll change the workings of my own mind,

Make the melancholy more,

Sick of sadness, sick of tears,

And a disease that has no cure.

Mistakes have piled to immeasurable,

One too many times I've cried,

Nothing seems to go away,

Despite everything I've tried.

If misery builds character,

If sadness makes us strong,

I should be good for something,

No matter that it seems so wrong.

Optimism is hard to find,

It's easier to doubt,

More realistic to just accept your fate,

Easier to go without.

Time heals all wounds, they say,

The past is just the past,

Just hold on tight,

Forgive, forget

The horror of today won't last.

(Right???)

<u>Countdown</u>

Your days have become numbered

Next breath will be your last,

For unforgivable circumstance

And what happened in the past.

Your stupid echoing laughter

Idiotic rambling tone,

Speak of things I cannot change

And things I don't condone.

Forget the "love" that we once knew,

Find solace in my hate,

Your suffering is my only bliss

The drug that doth sedate.

Make a mockery of my misery

Make a joke of my entity?

For every word you throw at me

A thousand more wait to burst free.

You think yourself amusing?

You have no right

All things boil down to this

Chaos, it comes tonight,

Take your chance and blow it.

Take your stand, then run,

You've no idea the hell I'll bring

Or the demon I can become.

In the Name Of

So long it's been

Too long, I fear,

Centuries have passed,

Perhaps you remember,

Hard to forget,

but

All good things don't last.

Never deny me, promise that,

It would be the end of me,

Everything else is gone,

And now you, too?

Hard to accept, but easy to see.

Acknowledge, please,

Inside at least,

Reality was once kind,

Rehearse if you must,

Don't forget,

Keep it fresh in your mind.

<u>*My Apologies*</u>

Forgive me for my altered state

Disregard me, please,

I was simply seeking something more,

Only wanted to appease.

Forgive my searching, eager eyes,

Ignore my blatant need,

So obvious, so intense,

Ignore me though I bleed.

Forgive me for my ignorance,

I assumed you'd understand,

You loved me once, I just thought

These things went hand in hand.

Look away as I cry, ignore the truth,

Pretend it's all okay,

You'll be fine, just move on,

Don't dare to lose your way.

I'm sorry for my naïve trust,

I'd go back there if I could,

To the days when you were someone else

And everything was good.

No more.

www.ingramcontent.com/pod-product-compliance
Lightning Source LLC
Chambersburg PA
CBHW080724120726
48001CB00010B/3141